MBA Professor

TRUST TO WIN

The Trust Blueprint of Successful Teams

BOOM
BUST
CYCLE

Make money in the Bubble

MBA Professor

While every precaution has been taken in the preparation of this book, the publisher assumes no responsibility for errors or omissions, or for damages resulting from the use of the information contained herein.

TRUST TO WIN: THE TRUST BLUEPRINT OF SUCCESSFUL TEAMS

First edition. December 14, 2024.

Copyright © 2024 Advanced Apologetics Research.

Written by Advanced Apologetics Research.

Table of Contents

Title Page

Copyright Page

1. Introduction to Economic Bubbles

2. The Anatomy of a Bubble

3. Phases of a Bubble

4. Historical Case Studies

5. Key Economic Theories and Models

6. Recognizing the Signs of a Bubble

7. Strategies to Capitalize on Bubbles

8. Surviving and Thriving Post-Burst

9. Ethics and Regulation

10. The Future of Bubbles in a Global Economy

11. Conclusion: Harnessing the Power of the Cycle

1. Introduction to Economic Bubbles

Definition and Overview

Economic bubbles refer to market phenomena characterized by the rapid escalation of asset prices to levels significantly higher than their intrinsic value, followed by a sharp decline. Bubbles are fuelled by exuberant market behaviour where speculation and optimism overshadow fundamental economic factors. These speculative frenzies often lead to unsustainable price levels that collapse once confidence dissipates.

Understanding Economic Bubbles

This document explores the defining characteristics of economic bubbles, their implications, and notable examples across various markets. Bubbles are phenomena that can lead to significant financial instability and have lasting effects on economies and societies. By examining the elements that constitute a bubble, we can better understand their formation, the behavior of market participants, and the aftermath of their inevitable corrections.

Defining Characteristics of Economic Bubbles

Excessive Price Inflation

Economic bubbles are often marked by a rapid increase in asset prices that is not supported by the underlying intrinsic value of those assets. This inflation is typically driven by speculative demand, where investors are motivated by the potential for quick profits rather than the fundamental worth of the assets themselves.

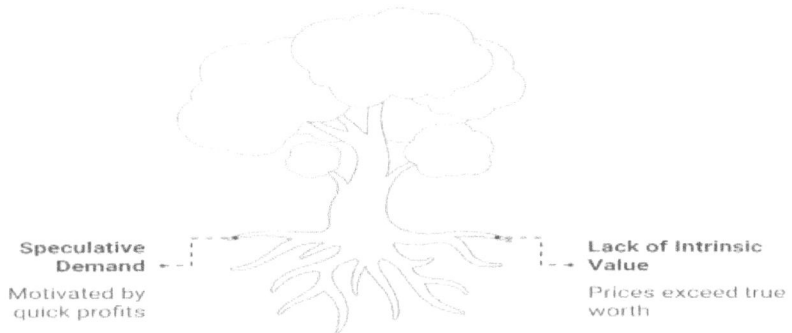

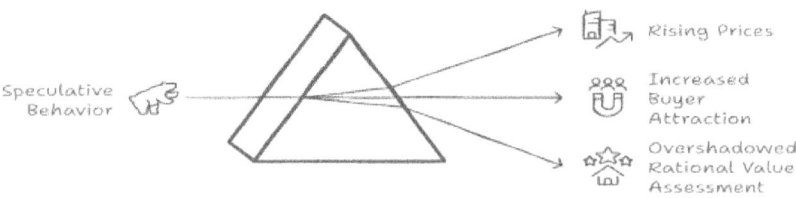

Speculative Behavior

In a bubble, market participants engage in speculative behavior, purchasing assets with the primary intention of selling them at a higher price in the future. This creates a feedback loop where rising prices attract more buyers, further inflating the bubble. The expectation of future price increases often overshadows rational assessments of value.

Correction Phase

Eventually, the market reaches a tipping point where the overvaluation becomes apparent. This leads to a sharp decline or "burst" of the bubble, resulting in significant losses for investors and a broader economic impact. The correction phase can be abrupt and severe, often catching many participants off guard.

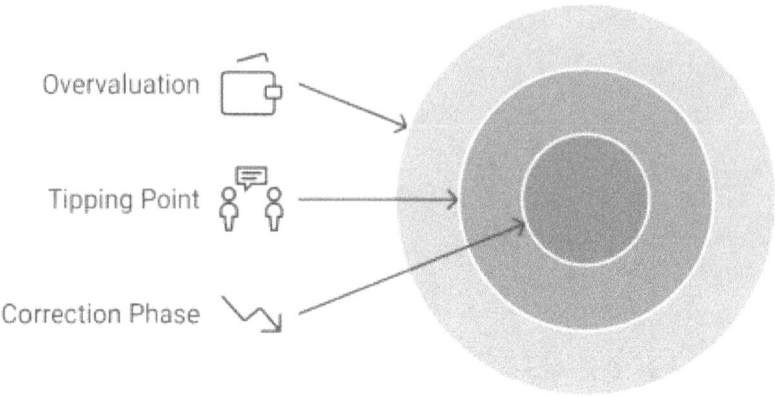

Key Examples of Economic Bubbles

1. **Housing Markets**: The housing bubble of the mid-2000s in the United States is a prime example, characterized by skyrocketing home prices fueled by easy credit and speculative buying. The subsequent crash led to widespread foreclosures and a prolonged economic downturn.

1. **Stock Markets**: The dot-com bubble of the late 1990s saw technology stocks soar to unsustainable levels based on speculative investments. The eventual burst resulted in significant losses for investors and a reevaluation of tech valuations.

1. **Commodities**: Bubbles can also occur in commodity markets, where prices may surge due to speculative trading rather than supply and demand fundamentals. The 2008 oil price spike is an example where prices soared before crashing back down.

1. **Cryptocurrencies**: The rapid rise and fall of cryptocurrencies, particularly Bitcoin, highlight the

speculative nature of digital assets. The volatility and dramatic price swings have led to discussions about the sustainability of such markets.

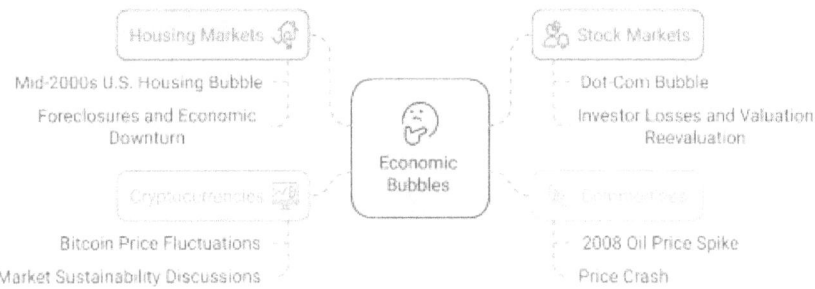

While not all economic booms culminate in a bust, the presence of bubbles can have profound and lasting economic and social consequences when they burst. Understanding the characteristics of bubbles, the behavior of market participants, and the historical context of notable examples can help investors and policymakers navigate the complexities of financial markets. Recognizing the signs of a bubble can be crucial in mitigating risks and preparing for potential corrections.

Historical Context of Boom-Bust Cycles

Boom-bust cycles have been a recurring theme in economic history, dating back centuries. They reflect the cyclical nature of markets, influenced by human psychology, economic policies, and structural imbalances.

Some notable historical bubbles include:

- **Tulip Mania (1630s)**: One of the first recorded speculative bubbles, where tulip bulb prices in the Netherlands reached extraordinary levels before crashing.
- **The South Sea Bubble (1720s)**: A speculative frenzy in Britain tied to the South Sea Company, where inflated stock prices led to devastating losses.

- **The Great Depression (1929)**: Fueled by stock market speculation and leverage, it ended in a historic financial collapse.
- **Dot-Com Bubble (1990s)**: The overvaluation of technology companies due to unrealistic growth expectations, leading to widespread losses in the early 2000s.

Understanding these historical cycles helps investors and policymakers anticipate potential warning signs of future bubbles and take measures to mitigate their effects.

Why Study Bubbles?

Studying bubbles is essential for several reasons:

1. **Economic Impact**: The burst of a bubble can cause significant financial loss, economic instability, and unemployment, as seen during the 2008 Global Financial Crisis.
2. **Behavioral Insights**: Bubbles expose human biases like herd mentality, overconfidence, and fear of missing out (FOMO), which distort rational decision-making.
3. **Policy Formulation**: Identifying the causes of bubbles helps governments and regulators design effective policies to minimize their occurrence and mitigate their impact.
4. **Investment Strategy**: Understanding the mechanics of bubbles enables investors to identify opportunities during boom periods while managing risks when a market shows signs of overvaluation.
5. **Systemic Risks**: Bubbles reveal vulnerabilities in financial systems, such as excessive leverage or inadequate regulation, which must be addressed to ensure long-term stability.

In essence, the study of economic bubbles provides valuable lessons for improving market efficiency, financial literacy, and economic resilience. By analyzing past patterns and understanding their implications, stakeholders can better navigate the cycles of booms and busts.

2. The Anatomy of a Bubble

Key Characteristics of Economic Bubbles

Economic bubbles follow a predictable set of features that distinguish them from regular market cycles. These include:

1. **Rapid Price Escalation**
   - Asset prices rise significantly over a short period, often with no proportional change in the underlying value or earnings.
   - Demand outstrips supply, creating an artificial scarcity and inflating prices further.
2. **Overvaluation**
   - Prices become disconnected from intrinsic value, driven by speculative buying rather than fundamental analysis.
   - Metrics such as price-to-earnings ratios or housing affordability indexes show extreme deviation from historical norms.
3. **High Trading Volume**
   - Speculative euphoria brings more participants into the market, leading to unprecedented levels of trading activity.
4. **Increased Leverage**
   - Participants often borrow heavily to invest, further inflating asset prices but increasing vulnerability when the market reverses.
5. **Unsustainable Growth**
   - The bubble depends on perpetual optimism and new buyers entering the market to sustain price growth.
   - Once new buyers dry up or sentiment shifts, the bubble begins to deflate.
6. **Inevitable Burst**

- Bubbles end when the market recognizes overvaluation, triggering panic selling and a rapid price collapse.
- This often leads to widespread financial losses, systemic risks, and economic downturns.

Rapid Price Escalation → Overvaluation → High Trading Volume → Increased Leverage → Unsustainable Growth → Inevitable Burst

The Psychological Drivers Behind Bubbles

Bubbles are fueled by human behavior, where psychological factors overpower rational decision-making. Key drivers include:

2. **Herd Mentality**
    a. Individuals follow the actions of others, assuming that the majority must be right. This collective behavior amplifies demand and inflates prices.
3. **Fear of Missing Out (FOMO)**
    a. Investors rush to buy assets due to the fear that they will miss out on future profits. This fear can override critical analysis and lead to irrational decisions.
4. **Overconfidence and Optimism Bias**
    a. Participants believe the market will continue to rise indefinitely, underestimating risks and overestimating their ability to time the market.
5. **Speculative Greed**
    a. The desire for quick profits drives speculative behavior, leading investors to disregard underlying fundamentals.
6. **Confirmation Bias**
    a. Investors seek out information that supports their belief in rising prices while ignoring warnings or negative indicators.

7. **Greater Fool Theory**
    a. Investors purchase overvalued assets, believing they can sell them to someone else at a higher price before the market collapses.

The Role of Media and Speculation

2. **Media Amplification**
    a. Media coverage plays a crucial role in fueling bubbles by creating hype around certain assets or markets.
    b. Sensationalized headlines and success stories attract more participants, reinforcing the narrative of endless growth.
3. **Market Speculation**
    a. Speculators, including traders and institutions, actively drive prices higher by buying with the intention of selling at a profit.
    b. Speculative trading leads to higher volatility and exaggerated price movements.
4. **Social Media and Influencers**
    a. In modern markets, platforms like Twitter, Reddit, and YouTube can create viral narratives that contribute to bubble formation (e.g., the GameStop saga).
5. **Echo Chambers**
    a. Online communities and forums can create feedback loops, where optimistic views dominate, and dissenting opinions are silenced or ignored.
6. **Celebrity Endorsements**
    a. High-profile endorsements of assets (e.g., cryptocurrencies) by celebrities and influencers can attract non-expert participants, further inflating the bubble.

By combining psychological drivers with media influence, bubbles gain momentum until the disconnect from reality becomes unsustainable. Understanding these dynamics is key to recognizing and responding to bubble conditions in real-time.

3. Phases of a Bubble

Economic bubbles typically follow a predictable life cycle, progressing through several distinct phases. Understanding these phases helps investors, policymakers, and businesses anticipate potential risks and opportunities.

1. Formation: The Beginning of the Boom

The formation phase marks the initial conditions that set the stage for a bubble. This phase is often subtle and hard to detect in real-time.

Key Drivers:

- **Favorable Economic Conditions**: Low-interest rates, strong economic growth, and abundant liquidity encourage investment.
- **Innovation or Paradigm Shift**: A new technology, product, or market opportunity generates excitement and optimism (e.g., the internet in the 1990s, cryptocurrencies in the 2010s).
- **Increased Demand**: Early adopters and savvy investors recognize the potential of an undervalued asset, triggering gradual price increases.
- **Media Attention**: Positive coverage begins to attract public interest and additional buyers.

Characteristics:

8. Prices begin to rise modestly, often supported by solid fundamentals.
9. Participation increases among knowledgeable investors and insiders.

2. Exponential Growth: Riding the Hype

During this phase, prices accelerate rapidly, and the bubble gains widespread attention. Speculation and enthusiasm drive market behavior.

Key Drivers:

7. **Speculative Buying**: Market participants buy assets not for their intrinsic value but for the expectation of selling at a higher price.
8. **Herd Mentality**: More individuals join the market, fearing they will miss out on profits (FOMO).
9. **Increased Leverage**: Borrowing becomes common as people seek to maximize their exposure to rising prices.
10. **Media and Influencer Hype**: Stories of large returns dominate headlines, further fueling demand.

Characteristics:

2. Asset prices rise at an unsustainable pace.
3. Trading volumes surge, and new market entrants (often inexperienced) join the frenzy.
4. Warning signs such as overvaluation and divergence from fundamentals start to emerge but are largely ignored.

3. The Peak: Irrational Exuberance

The peak represents the height of the bubble, where prices and sentiment reach their zenith. This phase is marked by euphoria and overconfidence, often described as "irrational exuberance" (a term coined by Alan Greenspan).

Key Drivers:

- **Widespread Participation**: Even conservative investors and skeptics join the market, driven by social pressure or greed.

- **Unrealistic Expectations**: Belief in perpetual price growth dominates market sentiment, with little regard for risks.
- **Media Frenzy**: Coverage reaches a fever pitch, often portraying the market as a "sure thing."

Characteristics:

6. Prices are at their highest, far exceeding intrinsic values.
7. The market shows signs of instability, with occasional volatility or corrections.
8. Insider selling may begin as savvy investors anticipate the crash.

---

4. The Collapse: Burst and Recovery

The collapse is triggered when the market recognizes overvaluation, and sentiment shifts from optimism to fear. This phase is often swift and severe.

Key Drivers:

- **Loss of Confidence**: Negative news or external shocks (e.g., policy changes, economic downturns) expose vulnerabilities.
- **Panic Selling**: Participants rush to exit the market, driving prices down rapidly.
- **Liquidity Crisis**: Overleveraged investors are forced to liquidate assets, exacerbating the downturn.

Characteristics:

- Prices plummet, often returning to or falling below pre-bubble levels.
- Financial losses cascade through the economy, affecting businesses, households, and institutions.
- Economic recessions or financial crises often follow, as seen in the aftermath of the 2008 housing bubble.

Recovery:

- After the collapse, the market gradually stabilizes, with prices reflecting fundamentals once again.
- Lessons are learned, but new bubbles often emerge in different sectors over time.

Visual Representation of a Bubble Lifecycle

- **Formation**: Steady rise in prices.
- **Exponential Growth**: Sharp upward curve.
- **Peak**: Highest point, with flat or erratic movements.
- **Collapse**: Rapid and steep decline.

By analyzing each phase, investors and policymakers can better prepare for the opportunities and risks associated with economic bubbles. Identifying the transition points between phases is particularly critical for managing investments and mitigating systemic risks.

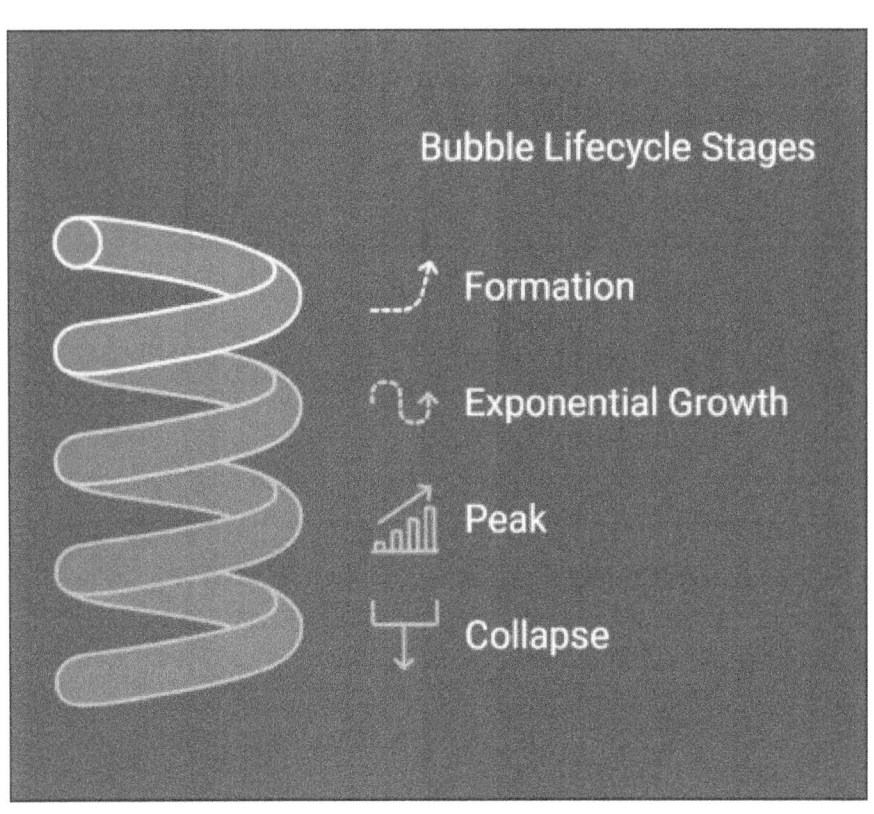

4. Historical Case Studies

Examining historical bubbles provides critical insights into how economic, psychological, and systemic factors contribute to their rise and fall. Below are four significant case studies that highlight different facets of bubble dynamics.

1. The Dutch Tulip Mania (1630s)

Often regarded as the first recorded economic bubble, the Dutch Tulip Mania illustrates the power of speculation and irrational exuberance in financial markets.

- **Background**:
  Tulips, introduced to the Netherlands in the late 16th century, became a luxury symbol among the wealthy. Rare tulip varieties, such as the Semper Augustus, were particularly prized.
- **The Bubble**:
  - Prices for tulip bulbs skyrocketed, with some bulbs selling for more than the price of a house.
  - Speculation intensified as traders used leverage to purchase bulbs, expecting to sell them at even higher prices.
  - The market expanded beyond wealthy merchants, attracting middle-class investors and even laborers.
- **The Collapse**:
  - In 1637, demand abruptly dried up, and prices plummeted.
  - Speculators were left holding worthless bulbs, leading to widespread financial losses.

- Though the economic impact was localized, Tulip Mania remains a cautionary tale about speculative excess.

2. The South Sea Bubble (1720s)

The South Sea Bubble highlights the dangers of overhyped financial schemes and the consequences of market manipulation.

10. **Background**:
    The South Sea Company was granted a monopoly on trade with South America in exchange for assuming a portion of Britain's national debt. The company promised vast riches, despite having limited trade prospects.
11. **The Bubble**:
    a. South Sea Company shares were aggressively promoted, leading to speculative buying.
    b. Prices rose by over 800% within months, fueled by widespread optimism and fraudulent practices.
    c. The frenzy extended to other speculative ventures, known as "bubble companies."
12. **The Collapse**:
    a. By late 1720, confidence eroded as insiders began selling their shares.
    b. Prices collapsed, wiping out investors and triggering economic turmoil.
    c. The scandal led to regulatory reforms, including stricter controls on joint-stock companies.

3. The Dot-Com Bubble (1990s-2000s)

The Dot-Com Bubble underscores the risks of overvaluing emerging technologies without understanding their long-term viability.

11. **Background**:
    The advent of the internet sparked a wave of innovation,

leading to the creation of numerous technology startups. Venture capital poured into companies with little to no revenue but significant "potential."

12. **The Bubble**:
    a. Investors bid up the stock prices of internet-related companies, some of which had no viable business models.
    b. The NASDAQ Composite Index rose by nearly 400% between 1995 and 2000.
    c. Companies spent lavishly on marketing and expansion, relying on investor funds rather than profits.
13. **The Collapse**:
    a. In 2000, the bubble burst as earnings failed to meet expectations, and valuations were questioned.
    b. The NASDAQ lost nearly 80% of its value by 2002, leading to mass bankruptcies of dot-com firms.
    c. While devastating, the bubble also paved the way for sustainable tech giants like Amazon and Google.

---

4. The Subprime Mortgage Crisis (2007-2008)

The Subprime Mortgage Crisis illustrates how systemic risk and financial engineering can amplify the consequences of a bubble.

5. **Background**:
   In the early 2000s, low-interest rates and lax lending standards fueled a housing boom in the United States. Subprime mortgages were issued to borrowers with poor credit, often packaged into mortgage-backed securities (MBS).
6. **The Bubble**:
   a. Home prices soared as demand surged, driven by speculative buying and predatory lending.
   b. Financial institutions heavily invested in MBS, underestimating the risks of default.

  c. Complex derivatives, such as collateralized debt obligations (CDOs), spread risk throughout the global financial system.
7. **The Collapse**:
  a. In 2007, rising interest rates and defaults exposed the fragility of the housing market.
  b. Home prices plummeted, and MBS values collapsed, leading to massive losses for banks and investors.
  c. The crisis triggered a global recession, resulting in government bailouts and sweeping regulatory reforms like the Dodd-Frank Act.

Comparative Analysis of Case Studies

Bubble	Drivers	Key Lessons
Tulip Mania (1630s)	Speculative demand for a luxury good	Avoid herd behavior and speculative greed
South Sea Bubble (1720s)	Overhyped schemes, market manipulation	Regulatory oversight is critical
Dot-Com Bubble (1990s)	Overvaluation of technology startups	Focus on fundamentals, not just potential
Subprime Crisis (2007-08)	Lax lending, systemic risk	Monitor leverage and financial innovation

Understanding these case studies helps identify patterns in bubble dynamics, offering critical lessons for investors, regulators, and policymakers to navigate and mitigate future bubbles effectively.

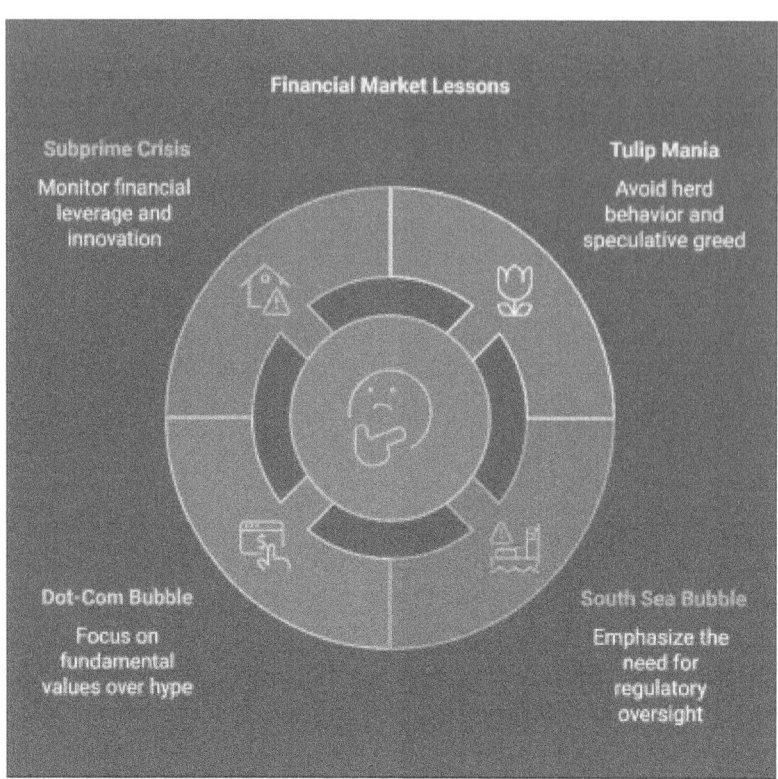

5. Key Economic Theories and Models

This chapter explores the theories and models that provide a framework for understanding the dynamics of economic bubbles, their formation, and eventual collapse. These frameworks also highlight the interplay between rational markets, psychological biases, and policy interventions.

1. Efficient Market Hypothesis (EMH) vs. Behavioral Economics

Efficient Market Hypothesis (EMH):

- The EMH, developed by Eugene Fama, posits that financial markets are "efficient," meaning asset prices fully reflect all available information at any given time.
- According to the EMH, bubbles should not occur because market participants rationally assess all information, preventing overvaluation or undervaluation of assets.
- **Implications for Bubbles**: Critics argue that EMH fails to account for psychological biases and irrational behaviors that lead to bubbles. Historical cases like the Dot-Com Bubble challenge the idea of consistently rational pricing.

Behavioral Economics:

13. Behavioral economics, championed by figures like Daniel Kahneman and Richard Thaler, challenges the rationality assumption of EMH. It studies how cognitive biases and emotions influence economic decisions.
14. **Key Behavioral Drivers in Bubbles**:
    a. **Herd Behavior**: Individuals follow the majority, assuming the crowd's actions are correct.
    b. **Overconfidence Bias**: Investors overestimate their ability to predict market movements.

c. **Loss Aversion**: Fear of missing out (FOMO) compels irrational investment decisions.

Comparison:

Aspect	EMH Perspective	Behavioral Economics Perspective
Market Efficiency	Prices reflect all available information	Markets are influenced by human irrationality
Bubble Explanation	Bubbles are anomalies	Bubbles result from psychological biases
Policy Implications	Minimal intervention	Regulation to mitigate human error

2. Market Speculation and Herd Behavior

Market Speculation:

14. Speculation involves buying assets with the expectation of profiting from price changes rather than their intrinsic value.
15. During bubbles, speculation creates self-reinforcing price increases, as investors buy simply because prices are rising.
16. Speculation is further amplified by financial instruments like leverage, derivatives, and short selling, which increase both returns and risks.

Herd Behavior:

8. Herd behavior is a collective psychological phenomenon where individuals mimic the actions of the majority.
9. **Drivers of Herd Behavior in Bubbles:**
    a. **Social Proof**: Investors interpret others' actions as correct and follow suit.
    b. **Fear of Missing Out (FOMO)**: Fear of being left out of potential profits pushes individuals to participate.

  c. **Echo Chambers**: Media, online forums, and influencers amplify consensus opinions, suppressing dissenting voices.

Implications:

- Herd behavior exacerbates price inflation during the boom phase and amplifies panic during the bust.
- Speculation and herd behavior feed off each other, creating a feedback loop that accelerates bubble dynamics.

---

3. The Role of Central Banks and Monetary Policy

Central banks and monetary policy play a dual role in bubble formation and prevention.

Bubble Formation:

9. **Loose Monetary Policy**: Low interest rates and excessive liquidity can fuel speculative investments by reducing borrowing costs.
   a. Example: The Federal Reserve's low rates during the early 2000s contributed to the housing bubble by making mortgages more accessible.
10. **Moral Hazard**: Market participants may take excessive risks if they believe central banks will intervene to stabilize markets (e.g., "too big to fail").

Bubble Mitigation and Burst Management:

- **Interest Rate Hikes**: Central banks may raise rates to cool overheated markets, though this can trigger a bubble's collapse.
- **Liquidity Provision**: During the burst, central banks provide liquidity to stabilize markets and prevent systemic failure.
    - Example: The Federal Reserve's quantitative easing (QE) programs post-2008 financial crisis.
- **Macroprudential Policies**: Central banks and regulators implement policies to address systemic risks, such as stricter lending standards and higher capital requirements for banks.

Challenges for Central Banks:

- **Recognizing Bubbles**: It is difficult to distinguish between rational price increases and speculative bubbles in real time.
- **Policy Timing**: Intervening too early can stifle growth, while acting too late can exacerbate the damage from a bubble burst.
- **Balancing Objectives**: Central banks must balance their mandate for price stability and employment with the need to prevent excessive risk-taking.

Key Insights and Policy Implications

- **Market Behavior**: Combining EMH's rational models with behavioral insights provides a more realistic understanding of bubbles.
- **Speculation Management**: Regulating speculative activities, such as margin lending and short selling, can help curb excessive risk-taking.
- **Role of Central Banks**: While monetary policy is a critical tool, central banks must coordinate with fiscal and regulatory policies to address bubbles effectively.

Understanding these theories and mechanisms equips policymakers, investors, and regulators to better navigate the complexities of economic bubbles and mitigate their adverse effects.

6. Recognizing the Signs of a Bubble

Identifying the signs of a bubble is critical for investors, regulators, and policymakers to mitigate risks and protect economic stability. This chapter examines key indicators and warning signs that suggest markets may be entering bubble territory, as well as the challenges of predicting the peak.

1. Market Indicators of Overvaluation

1. **Price-to-Earnings (P/E) Ratios**
   - When P/E ratios for stocks or sectors are significantly higher than historical averages, it indicates overvaluation.
   - Example: During the Dot-Com Bubble, P/E ratios of tech stocks soared to unsustainable levels.
2. **Housing Affordability Index**
   - In housing markets, a sharp increase in home prices relative to incomes or rents suggests a bubble.
   - Example: The Subprime Mortgage Crisis saw home prices far outpacing income growth.
3. **Asset Price Acceleration**
   - A steep, exponential rise in asset prices over a short period often signals speculative buying.
4. **Low Dividend Yields**
   - For stocks, low or nonexistent dividend yields can indicate that prices are driven more by speculation than earnings.
5. **Leverage and Credit Growth**
   - Rapid growth in borrowing, especially for speculative purposes, inflates bubbles.
   - Example: Excessive leverage during the 2008 crisis exacerbated losses when the bubble burst.

2. Common Warning Signs of Market Instability

15. **Irrational Exuberance**
    a. Coined by Alan Greenspan, this refers to widespread overconfidence and belief that prices will rise indefinitely, despite weak fundamentals.
16. **Herd Behavior**
    a. When the majority of market participants exhibit similar buying behavior, driven by fear of missing out (FOMO) or social proof, instability looms.
17. **Over-Reliance on Debt**
    a. High levels of margin trading, speculative loans, or subprime lending create systemic vulnerabilities.
18. **Speculative Investments**
    a. Markets dominated by speculative activity (e.g., flipping houses, meme stock trading) show signs of instability.
19. **New or Unfamiliar Asset Classes**
    a. Bubbles often form around new technologies, industries, or asset classes, such as dot-com startups in the 1990s or cryptocurrencies in the 2010s.
20. **Media Hype and Public Frenzy**
    a. Extensive media coverage, along with stories of ordinary people making extraordinary profits, signals growing speculation.
21. **Weak Regulatory Oversight**
    a. Lax regulations often coincide with bubbles, as seen in the subprime lending practices leading up to the 2008 crisis.

3. Predicting the Peak

Predicting the exact peak of a bubble is notoriously difficult because of the dynamic and often irrational nature of markets. However, there are some strategies and indicators that provide guidance:

17. **Market Sentiment Reversal**
    a. A shift from optimism to fear often precedes the peak.
    b. Example: Insider selling, negative news, or increasing skepticism from analysts.
18. **Extreme Valuation Metrics**
    a. When valuation metrics (e.g., P/E ratios, price-to-book ratios) reach unprecedented highs, the market may be near a peak.
19. **Divergence from Fundamentals**
    a. A disconnect between asset prices and economic indicators (e.g., GDP growth, corporate earnings) often suggests the bubble is unsustainable.
20. **Volatility and Correction Signs**
    a. Markets may experience sharp, short-term corrections or increased volatility as speculative buying wanes.
21. **Over-Participation by Novice Investors**
    a. A surge in participation by inexperienced investors, lured by media hype, indicates the market is overextended.
    b. Example: Retail investors flooding into meme stocks like GameStop in 2021.
22. **Liquidity Tightening**
    a. Central bank actions, such as interest rate hikes or reduced monetary stimulus, often act as a trigger for bubble bursts.

Challenges in Recognizing and Acting on Bubbles

10. **The "This Time Is Different" Fallacy**
    a. Participants often rationalize overvaluation by arguing that current conditions (e.g., new technologies, global markets) make traditional metrics irrelevant.
11. **Delayed Reactions**
    a. Even when warning signs are evident, markets can remain irrational longer than anticipated, creating a false sense of security.

12. **Economic and Political Pressure**
    a. Policymakers and regulators may hesitate to act decisively against bubbles due to fear of disrupting growth or facing backlash.
13. **Timing Risks for Investors**
    a. Exiting the market too early may lead to missed gains, while exiting too late can result in significant losses.

Conclusion

Recognizing the signs of a bubble requires a combination of quantitative analysis, psychological insights, and vigilance. While predicting the exact peak remains a challenge, monitoring indicators such as overvaluation, speculative behavior, and systemic vulnerabilities can provide critical early warnings. For investors and policymakers alike, maintaining a disciplined approach is key to navigating the risks and opportunities of market bubbles.

7. Strategies to Capitalize on Bubbles

While bubbles pose significant risks, they also present opportunities for savvy investors who can navigate their dynamics effectively. This chapter outlines strategies for capitalizing on bubbles, managing risks, and exiting profitably before a market collapse.

1. Investing in the Boom Phase

The boom phase of a bubble offers high returns as asset prices skyrocket. However, it requires a disciplined and informed approach to maximize gains while minimizing risks.

Key Strategies:

1. **Focus on Momentum Investing**
   - Invest in assets experiencing strong upward trends, as they often outperform during bubbles.
   - Use technical indicators like moving averages or relative strength to identify momentum.
2. **Diversify Within the Bubble**
   - Avoid concentrating investments in a single asset or sector. Spread your exposure across various high-growth assets within the bubble.
   - Example: During the Dot-Com Bubble, investors who diversified across multiple tech stocks were better positioned than those who focused on one company.
3. **Limit Exposure**
   - Allocate a portion of your portfolio to bubble investments while keeping the rest in safer assets. This balances potential gains with risk mitigation.
4. **Follow Insider Activity**

- o Monitor insider transactions. If company executives are buying, it could indicate confidence in the growth phase.
5. **Ride the "Early Majority" Wave**
    - o Invest during the early to mid-stage of the bubble when prices are rising but not yet at extreme levels. Avoid entering too late, as risks increase near the peak.

---

2. Hedging Risks During Uncertain Times

As bubbles mature, the risk of collapse grows. Investors must employ strategies to protect their capital and minimize losses.

Key Strategies:

22. **Use Stop-Loss Orders**
    a. Set stop-loss orders to automatically sell assets if prices fall below a certain threshold. This prevents emotional decision-making during volatile periods.
23. **Diversify Across Asset Classes**
    a. Reduce exposure to the bubble by investing in uncorrelated assets such as bonds, commodities, or international markets.
    b. Example: During the housing bubble, investors with exposure to gold or government bonds experienced fewer losses.
24. **Implement Options Strategies**
    a. Buy put options to hedge against potential declines in bubble assets.
    b. Example: Investors in tech stocks during the Dot-Com Bubble could have used put options to limit losses during the crash.
25. **Monitor Macro Indicators**
    a. Watch for early warning signs such as rising interest rates, tightening liquidity, or economic slowdowns that may signal the bubble is nearing its end.
26. **Maintain Liquidity**

a. Keep a portion of your portfolio in cash or liquid assets to take advantage of buying opportunities after the bubble bursts.

---

3. Timing Your Exit: Cashing Out Before the Burst

Exiting a bubble at the right time is crucial to locking in profits and avoiding significant losses.

Key Strategies:

23. **Set Profit Targets**
    a. Define clear exit points based on predetermined profit levels or valuation metrics.
    b. Example: If an asset's price doubles your investment, sell a portion to secure profits while leaving some exposure for potential further gains.
24. **Watch for Sentiment Shifts**
    a. Pay attention to changes in market sentiment, such as increasing skepticism, negative news, or insider selling. These often precede a downturn.
25. **Scale Out Gradually**
    a. Instead of selling your entire position at once, sell incrementally as prices rise. This reduces the risk of exiting too early or too late.
26. **Analyze Fundamentals**
    a. Exit when the asset's price deviates significantly from its intrinsic value or when growth expectations become unrealistic.
    b. Example: Investors in the housing bubble could have exited as home prices became unaffordable relative to incomes.
27. **Leverage Historical Patterns**
    a. Use lessons from past bubbles to gauge when a market may be nearing its peak. For instance, extreme valuation metrics or widespread speculative behavior often signal the top.
28. **Act Contrarian**

a. When euphoria reaches extreme levels, consider reducing exposure. This contrarian approach often aligns with the market's peak.
b. Example: Warren Buffett's adage, "Be fearful when others are greedy," applies well in bubble conditions.

Balancing Risks and Rewards

Phase	Goal	Strategy
Early Boom Phase	Enter strategically	Invest in high-growth sectors/assets
Mid to Late Boom	Maximize profits, limit risk	Use stop-loss orders, diversify exposure
Pre-Collapse	Exit profitably	Scale out, monitor sentiment, hedge risks
Post-Collapse	Re-enter selectively	Buy undervalued assets during recovery

Conclusion

Capitalizing on bubbles requires a combination of calculated risk-taking, disciplined investing, and proactive risk management. By recognizing the boom phase, hedging effectively, and timing exits carefully, investors can maximize returns while protecting their portfolios from the devastating effects of a bubble burst. Understanding historical patterns and market dynamics is essential for making informed decisions in these volatile environments.

8. Surviving and Thriving Post-Burst

The aftermath of a bubble's collapse can be financially and emotionally challenging. However, with the right strategies, investors can mitigate losses, capitalize on recovery opportunities, and build resilience for future market cycles.

1. Managing Financial Losses

The immediate priority post-burst is to assess and stabilize your financial situation.

Key Strategies:

1. **Assess Portfolio Damage**
   - Analyze your holdings to determine the extent of losses. Identify which assets are worth holding and which should be sold.
   - Focus on long-term investments with strong fundamentals that are likely to recover.
2. **Rebalance Your Portfolio**
   - Diversify your holdings to reduce concentration in volatile sectors.
   - Allocate funds across asset classes like equities, bonds, and cash to rebuild stability.
3. **Avoid Panic Selling**
   - Resist the urge to liquidate your portfolio during market turmoil. History shows that markets often recover over time.
   - Example: Investors who held through the 2008 financial crisis recouped losses as markets rebounded.
4. **Reduce Leverage**
   - If you used borrowed funds, prioritize paying off high-interest debt to avoid compounding losses.

- Refrain from taking on new leverage until markets stabilize.
5. **Review Financial Goals**
    - Reevaluate your investment strategy and timelines to align with current market conditions.
    - Be prepared to adjust short-term goals without compromising long-term objectives.

---

2. Identifying Recovery Opportunities

Bubbles often leave behind undervalued assets and opportunities for long-term growth.

Key Strategies:

27. **Seek Out Quality Assets**
    a. Focus on assets that were oversold during the collapse but have strong fundamentals and growth potential.
    b. Example: After the Dot-Com Bubble, companies like Amazon and eBay rebounded and became industry leaders.
28. **Invest in Counter-Cyclical Sectors**
    a. Consider sectors that tend to perform well during economic downturns, such as consumer staples, utilities, and healthcare.
29. **Look for Consolidation Trends**
    a. Post-bubble periods often lead to industry consolidation, where stronger companies acquire weaker ones. Invest in market leaders with robust balance sheets.
30. **Capitalize on Distressed Assets**
    a. Explore opportunities in distressed real estate, stocks, or bonds that can offer high returns during recovery.
    b. Example: During the 2008 housing crisis, investors who purchased undervalued properties achieved significant gains in the following years.
31. **Monitor Policy Responses**

a. Governments and central banks often implement stimulus measures post-burst, such as quantitative easing or infrastructure spending. Position your investments to benefit from these initiatives.

3. Lessons from the Past for Future Investments

Each bubble and subsequent crash offers valuable lessons for developing a resilient investment approach.

Key Lessons:

29. **Focus on Fundamentals**
    a. Avoid speculative assets that lack clear intrinsic value or revenue models.
    b. Example: Dot-Com investors learned the importance of profitability over hype.
30. **Maintain Diversification**
    a. A diversified portfolio reduces the impact of a bubble collapse on overall wealth.
    b. Include uncorrelated assets like bonds, gold, or international equities to spread risk.
31. **Recognize Red Flags**
    a. Be vigilant for signs of overvaluation, such as skyrocketing prices, high P/E ratios, and excessive leverage.
    b. Monitor sentiment indicators like euphoria and media hype, which often signal a peak.
32. **Embrace Risk Management**
    a. Use stop-loss orders, options, or hedging strategies to protect against downside risks during volatile markets.
33. **Think Long-Term**
    a. Invest with a horizon of 5–10 years to ride out market cycles and avoid the pitfalls of short-term speculation.
    b. Example: Long-term investors in the S&P 500 consistently outperform those who try to time the market.

34. **Learn from History**
    a. Study past bubbles to understand patterns and avoid repeating mistakes. Each bubble, from Tulip Mania to the Subprime Crisis, underscores the importance of disciplined investing.

From Survival to Growth: A Roadmap Post-Burst

Phase	Goal	Action Plan
Immediate Post-Burst	Stabilize finances	Assess losses, reduce leverage, rebalance
Mid-Term Recovery	Identify growth opportunities	Invest in undervalued assets, monitor policies
Long-Term Planning	Build resilience	Diversify, focus on fundamentals, manage risk

---

Conclusion

Recovering from a bubble collapse requires a combination of short-term damage control and long-term strategic planning. By focusing on quality assets, maintaining a disciplined investment approach, and learning from past bubbles, investors can not only survive but thrive in the aftermath. Market resilience and economic cycles will continue to create opportunities for those prepared to navigate them wisely.

9. Ethics and Regulation

Economic bubbles pose not only financial risks but also ethical dilemmas and systemic challenges. Understanding the moral implications of speculation, the responsibilities of governments and financial institutions, and how regulations can mitigate risks is crucial for fostering a stable and equitable financial system.

1. Moral Implications of Speculation

Speculation is a double-edged sword in financial markets. While it provides liquidity and price discovery, it can also exacerbate bubbles and lead to harmful societal consequences.

Key Ethical Issues:

1. **Exploitation of Vulnerabilities**
   - Speculators often exploit uninformed or less experienced investors, fueling unsustainable price increases.
   - Example: During the Subprime Mortgage Crisis, predatory lenders targeted low-income borrowers with risky loans.
2. **Wealth Inequality**
   - Bubbles disproportionately benefit wealthy individuals and institutions, who have more resources to speculate and hedge risks. When bubbles burst, the broader public often bears the economic fallout.
3. **Moral Hazard**
   - Speculators may take excessive risks, assuming that governments or central banks will intervene to prevent market collapses.
   - Example: The concept of "too big to fail" during the 2008 financial crisis created a perception that large

institutions would be bailed out, encouraging reckless behavior.
4. **Resource Misallocation**
    - Speculative bubbles divert capital from productive uses (e.g., innovation or infrastructure) to unproductive activities driven by short-term profit motives.
5. **Public Confidence and Trust**
    - Bubbles and crashes erode trust in financial markets, as they expose systemic weaknesses and unethical practices. This can deter long-term investments critical for economic growth.

---

2. The Role of Government and Financial Institutions

Governments and financial institutions play a pivotal role in managing the risks associated with bubbles. Their actions (or inactions) can significantly influence the formation, escalation, or mitigation of bubbles.

Government Responsibilities:

32. **Ensuring Market Transparency**
    a. Governments must mandate disclosure of accurate and timely information to enable informed decision-making by investors.
33. **Promoting Financial Literacy**
    a. Public education on financial markets helps reduce speculative behavior driven by misinformation or hype.
34. **Addressing Systemic Risks**
    a. Governments must monitor and mitigate systemic risks, such as excessive leverage or interconnections between financial institutions.

Role of Central Banks:

35. **Monetary Policy**

       a. Central banks influence market conditions through interest rates and liquidity.
       b. Example: Raising interest rates during overheated markets can reduce speculative borrowing.
36. **Macroprudential Regulation**
       a. Central banks can enforce capital requirements, stress testing, and leverage limits to ensure the stability of financial institutions.

Financial Institutions' Responsibilities:

14. **Ethical Conduct**
       a. Banks, investment firms, and other institutions must prioritize ethical practices, such as avoiding conflicts of interest and ensuring the suitability of financial products for clients.
15. **Responsible Lending and Underwriting**
       a. Financial institutions should avoid issuing loans or securities with excessive risk, as seen during the Subprime Mortgage Crisis.

---

3. How Regulations Can Prevent Bubbles

Regulations are essential for curbing speculative excess and minimizing the systemic risks of bubbles. Effective regulatory frameworks should strike a balance between fostering innovation and maintaining market stability.

Key Regulatory Measures:

- **Leverage and Margin Controls**
    - Limit borrowing and margin trading to reduce the amplification of speculative bubbles.
    - Example: The Federal Reserve's margin requirements helped curb speculative excess in the aftermath of the Great Depression.
- **Stricter Lending Standards**

- o Ensure that loans are issued based on the borrower's ability to repay, rather than inflated asset prices.
- o Example: Post-2008 reforms, such as the Dodd-Frank Act, introduced tighter mortgage underwriting standards.
- **Market Surveillance**
    - o Monitor trading activity for signs of manipulation or excessive speculation, and enforce penalties for unethical practices.
- **Disclosure and Transparency**
    - o Require detailed disclosures from companies and financial institutions about their risks and exposures.
    - o Example: Enhanced reporting requirements for derivatives and complex financial products under the Basel III framework.
- **Capital and Liquidity Requirements**
    - o Mandate financial institutions to hold sufficient capital to absorb losses during downturns, reducing the risk of collapse.
- **Regulation of Emerging Markets**
    - o Introduce guidelines for new asset classes, such as cryptocurrencies, to prevent unchecked speculation.
    - o Example: Governments worldwide are implementing regulations for cryptocurrency exchanges to address risks of volatility and fraud.

Challenges in Regulation:

11. **Global Coordination**
    a. In a globalized financial system, regulations must be harmonized across countries to prevent regulatory arbitrage.
12. **Balancing Innovation and Stability**
    a. Overregulation can stifle innovation, while underregulation may allow bubbles to form unchecked.
13. **Regulatory Capture**

a. Policymakers may be influenced by industry lobbying, leading to lenient regulations that fail to address risks.

Conclusion

Ethics and regulation are integral to preventing and mitigating economic bubbles. Governments, central banks, and financial institutions must work collaboratively to implement robust regulatory frameworks, promote transparency, and uphold ethical standards. By addressing the root causes of bubbles and fostering public trust in financial markets, the cycle of boom and bust can be managed more effectively.

10. The Future of Bubbles in a Global Economy

Economic bubbles will continue to shape global markets as technology, innovation, and interconnected economies create new opportunities and risks. Understanding how these factors influence bubble formation and preparing for the next boom-bust cycle is critical for investors, policymakers, and businesses.

1. How Technology Impacts Bubble Formation

1.1 Acceleration of Information Flow

- Technology enables the rapid dissemination of information (and misinformation), amplifying speculative behavior.
- Social media platforms and online forums create echo chambers, where hype spreads quickly and fuels demand for overvalued assets.
- Example: The 2021 GameStop saga, where Reddit-fueled retail trading led to a stock price surge disconnected from fundamentals.

1.2 Algorithmic Trading and AI

35. High-frequency trading (HFT) and algorithmic strategies can exacerbate volatility, as machines react instantaneously to price changes.
36. While AI offers insights for price prediction, it can also lead to herd-like behavior when similar algorithms dominate trading.

1.3 Democratization of Investing

37. Digital platforms and apps, such as Robinhood, have made investing more accessible, leading to increased participation by inexperienced retail investors.
38. This democratization can magnify speculative bubbles, as seen with meme stocks and cryptocurrencies.

1.4 Emerging Technologies as Catalysts

16. Breakthrough technologies (e.g., artificial intelligence, blockchain, electric vehicles) often trigger speculative cycles due to their transformative potential.
17. Example: The Dot-Com Bubble was driven by overhyped internet technologies, many of which lacked viable business models at the time.

2. Cryptocurrencies and Emerging Markets

2.1 Cryptocurrencies and Digital Assets

- Cryptocurrencies like Bitcoin and Ethereum represent a new asset class with high potential for speculative bubbles.
- **Bubble Characteristics in Crypto Markets:**
    - Extreme price volatility.
    - Retail-driven speculation fueled by social media and influencer endorsements.
    - Limited regulatory oversight, making markets prone to manipulation.
- Example: Bitcoin's meteoric rise in 2017 and subsequent crash showcased the speculative nature of cryptocurrency markets.

2.2 NFTs and the Token Economy

14. Non-fungible tokens (NFTs) have emerged as speculative assets, with prices for digital art and collectibles reaching exorbitant levels.
15. The lack of intrinsic value and dependence on hype make NFTs particularly vulnerable to bubble dynamics.

2.3 Emerging Markets and Financial Instability

- Emerging markets often attract speculative capital due to high growth potential but can quickly reverse during global economic shocks.
- Example: The Asian Financial Crisis (1997) was partially driven by speculative inflows into emerging markets, followed by a sudden outflow of capital.
- **Technology's Role in Emerging Markets:**
    - Mobile banking and fintech adoption have increased financial access but also introduced risks of speculative bubbles in less-regulated markets.

---

3. Preparing for the Next Boom-Bust Cycle

3.1 Identifying Potential Catalysts

- **Technological Innovations**: Breakthroughs in AI, quantum computing, biotech, or renewable energy could drive the next bubble.
- **Monetary Policy**: Prolonged periods of low interest rates and quantitative easing can inflate asset prices.
- **Geopolitical Shifts**: Trade wars, deglobalization, or economic realignments could create speculative opportunities in certain sectors or regions.

3.2 Strengthening Regulation

- Governments and regulators must anticipate risks associated with new technologies and asset classes.
- Example: Introducing comprehensive rules for cryptocurrencies, including taxation, anti-money laundering measures, and investor protections.

3.3 Enhancing Financial Literacy

- Education on investment principles, market risks, and behavioral biases can help individuals make informed decisions and reduce speculative excess.

3.4 Scenario Planning for Investors

- **Diversification**: Maintain a balanced portfolio with exposure to multiple asset classes.
- **Risk Assessment**: Regularly evaluate market conditions and stress-test portfolios for potential downturns.
- **Liquidity Management**: Keep a portion of assets in liquid forms to take advantage of post-burst recovery opportunities.

3.5 Building Institutional Resilience

- Central banks and financial institutions must develop tools to detect and manage systemic risks in real time.
- Example: Using AI to monitor asset price trends, leverage ratios, and cross-border capital flows for early signs of bubble formation.

Future Outlook: Navigating Global Bubbles

The global economy will continue to face bubble cycles as innovation, speculative behavior, and interconnected markets evolve. While technology and emerging asset classes create opportunities, they also introduce risks that must be carefully managed.

Key Takeaways:

- **Proactive Regulation**: Policymakers must anticipate risks associated with technological advances and speculative behaviors.
- **Investor Preparedness**: Financial literacy, diversification, and disciplined investing are crucial for navigating speculative markets.

- **Global Coordination**: Cross-border collaboration among regulators is essential to address bubbles in interconnected markets.

By understanding the drivers of future bubbles and preparing for the next cycle, stakeholders can mitigate risks while capitalizing on opportunities in a rapidly changing economic landscape.

11. Conclusion: Harnessing the Power of the Cycle

Economic bubbles, while often destructive, also offer valuable lessons and opportunities for those who understand their dynamics. This chapter consolidates insights from historical trends, strategies for resilience, and approaches to capitalize on opportunities while managing risks effectively.

1. Key Takeaways from Historical Trends

Historical bubbles have consistently followed similar patterns, offering clear lessons for navigating future cycles:

1. **Common Phases**
   - Bubbles generally progress through the same stages: formation, exponential growth, peak, and collapse. Recognizing these phases early provides a strategic advantage.
   - Example: Identifying the "irrational exuberance" stage during the Dot-Com Bubble allowed some investors to exit before the collapse.
2. **Psychological Drivers Matter**
   - Behavioral biases, such as herd mentality, fear of missing out (FOMO), and overconfidence, drive speculative excess.
   - Lesson: Maintaining a rational, data-driven perspective can protect against emotional decisions.
3. **Innovation and Hype**
   - Bubbles often form around transformative technologies or industries, such as railroads, the internet, or cryptocurrencies.

- Lesson: Focus on distinguishing genuine long-term value from overhyped trends.
4. **Systemic Risks Exacerbate Crises**
    - Excessive leverage, interconnected financial systems, and lax regulation amplify the damage when bubbles burst.
    - Lesson: Monitoring systemic vulnerabilities is crucial for investors and policymakers alike.
5. **Recovery Opportunities Exist**
    - Post-burst periods often leave behind undervalued assets with strong fundamentals, offering long-term growth potential.
    - Lesson: Stay prepared to invest in recovery opportunities rather than focusing solely on short-term losses.

---

2. Building a Resilient Financial Strategy

A resilient financial strategy is essential for navigating bubbles while mitigating risks and capitalizing on opportunities.

Key Components of Resilience:

37. **Diversification**
    a. Spread investments across asset classes, sectors, and geographic regions to reduce risk concentration.
    b. Include counter-cyclical assets like bonds, gold, or dividend-paying stocks to cushion against volatility.
38. **Disciplined Risk Management**
    a. Set stop-loss orders, use hedging strategies, and avoid excessive leverage to protect capital.
    b. Regularly reassess your portfolio to ensure alignment with market conditions and long-term goals.
39. **Focus on Fundamentals**
    a. Prioritize investments in companies or assets with strong earnings, sustainable business models, and realistic valuations.

        b. Example: Post-Dot-Com, Amazon emerged as a survivor due to its solid growth trajectory, while many speculative companies failed.
40. **Liquidity Management**
        a. Maintain a portion of assets in liquid form to capitalize on opportunities during market downturns or recoveries.
41. **Long-Term Perspective**
        a. Avoid short-term speculation and focus on building wealth over multiple market cycles.
        b. Example: Investors who held through the 2008 crisis saw significant recovery in global markets over the following decade.

---

3. Navigating the Opportunities and Challenges of Bubbles

Bubbles present both risks and opportunities. A strategic approach can help navigate the challenges while reaping potential benefits.

Opportunities:

39. **Early Entry During Formation**
        a. Investing during the early stages of a bubble can yield high returns before speculative excess takes over.
        b. Example: Early investors in cryptocurrencies like Bitcoin (before 2016) realized substantial gains as adoption grew.
40. **Identifying Post-Burst Bargains**
        a. After a bubble bursts, markets often overcorrect, leaving valuable assets undervalued.
        b. Example: Investors who bought real estate after the 2008 housing crash saw significant appreciation in subsequent years.
41. **Technological Transformations**
        a. Bubbles often occur in industries poised for long-term growth, providing opportunities for investment in genuine innovation.

Challenges:

18. **Timing the Peak**
    a. Predicting the peak of a bubble is extremely difficult, making it challenging to maximize gains and avoid losses.
    b. Solution: Use incremental exit strategies to lock in profits gradually.
19. **Emotional Biases**
    a. The psychological pressures of herd behavior and FOMO can lead to poor decision-making.
    b. Solution: Maintain a disciplined, evidence-based approach to investing.
20. **Systemic Risks**
    a. Bubbles can destabilize entire economies, impacting even well-diversified portfolios.
    b. Solution: Monitor macroeconomic indicators and adjust your strategy proactively.

Final Thoughts: Harnessing the Power of the Cycle

Bubbles are an inherent part of economic cycles, driven by human behavior, innovation, and market dynamics. While they bring risks of financial instability, they also offer significant opportunities for growth and wealth creation.

By studying historical patterns, developing a resilient financial strategy, and preparing for both booms and busts, individuals and institutions can navigate these cycles effectively. The key is to remain vigilant, disciplined, and adaptable, recognizing that every bubble—while unique—offers lessons for a more informed and strategic approach to investing.

As the global economy evolves, those who learn to harness the power of bubbles will not only survive market volatility but thrive in the opportunities it creates.

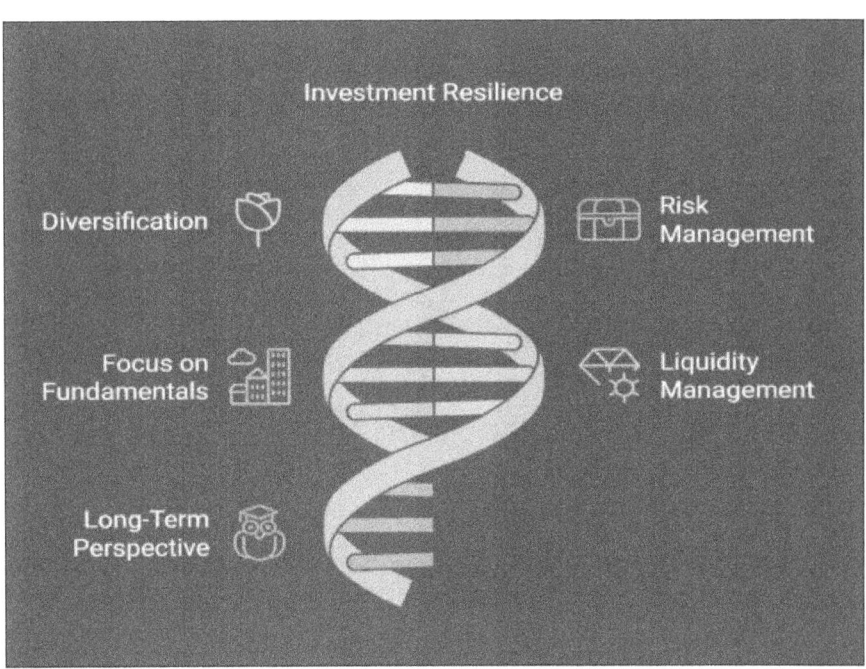

www.ingramcontent.com/pod-product-compliance
Lightning Source LLC
Chambersburg PA
CBHW070420230526
45471CB00006B/2896